TAP INTO *YOUR* DESTINY

by J. White

TAP INTO *YOUR* DESTINY
© 2009 by Jerry White
ISBN-978-0-615-31402-0

Printed in the United States of America

Table of Contents

TAP 10- DANCING WITH THE STARS

TAP 11- REJECTION IS A BLESSING

TAP 12- ANOTHER DIVINE APPOINTMENT

Dedication

This book is dedicated to Jada Akilah Thompson White who has been the best friend and support that a person could ask for. You are like the seventh day of God's creation in that you've given me rest and allowed me to come closer into the fullness of who I am. My journey with you has prepared me for the days ahead. Through what you've given me, I now see it illuminated in your life. Your belief in me keeps a place in my heart that cannot be penetrated. Thank you for helping me tap into the strength I need to live my Destiny.

Special thanks: to my sister Linia (Triumph) who tapped into your creativity long before I did. You've influenced me in so many ways and I want you to know that your courage to be different has always shined so bright to me. You are changing lives just by your presence.

Yvonne, you are one of the kindest people I've ever met. I've *seen* you care for people in ways that many "believers" talk about. You are the one person on this earth that I can sit with and just burst out into sincere gut-wrenching laughter for absolutely no reason at all. Thank you for always being the same.

Faheem, if you've ever doubted me, you've never shown it. You are and always have been down for whatever and I consider you to be one of my closest friends. Who would've known that one day in the barbershop would knit us together for this lifetime?

Al CaJones (Broadway), Thank you for taking the time to get to know me and always listen with an ear out for my best interest. Watching your evolution has been motivating in my life and I appreciate you for just being you. Even if "you ain't no cop J-Reed."

Donnie G, you have been a friend but more importantly, you have been an example. An example of how to be spiritual and not religious! Thank you for being a living example of balance.

Aunt Roz, you've been the glue that has held our family together and I appreciate the value in that. You genuinely want the best for people and that is a trait so uncommon in a "me me me" world.

Alfrieda (mom), you have a love for me that is so rare, it's hard to put into words. You are the most thoughtful person I've ever met. You "wow" me with your love.

Big Amos, when I look at you I see a man that refuses to quit. You have such a great perspective on life and I thank you for always laughing.

Emmanuel (Mani), Your love and support for me has been genuine from the first day we met at the park. I knew we were going to be friends forever that day. You and Teri have been safe havens when the storm beat in my life.

Lafayette (Ray Ray), I don't know if I've ever met a man so focused on God. You are a walking example of Christ and I look up to you as an example.

Coriya (Burnstein), You are wise beyond your years. I thank you for your sincerity and ministry. Watching you navigate through life with Bryce has helped me to see nuggets of how my mother made it.

Sean and Jon, you both inspired me to learn tap and you two continue to teach me via the internet.

Barbara and Cynthia, you were my family away from my family. You are two Angels God strategically placed in my life.

Jason Young, you are a true brother in Christ. When I was at my darkest hour, you and your wife encouraged me without judgment and I am grateful for a friend like you.

The Johnson Family, from the time I could walk, I've been able to walk into your house as if it were my own. Each one of you are family to me and the foundation you helped lay, is a major part of who I am today.

Noel Jones, my walk with God truly began while sitting under your teaching. You helped take my life to another level.

Tony (Lowkster), It takes a special person to keep my mother laughing and she just gets a kick out of you. Watching you has given me a greater appreciation for patience.

Jerry White Senior, thank you for passing down your creative eye and passion for young people. I started taking kids around the country because I lived it through you.

Finally and most phenomenally mom (CaLynn, Lerley), there really aren't enough pens in the world to write about my gratitude to and for you. I often reflect on your journey whenever I need strength. You are the most beautiful woman I've ever seen. Your love, compassion and generosity is so humbling to me. No matter where the sun is, it's always shining. You represent both the sun and the son to me. For that I'm grateful. Don't ever allow anyone or anything to quench your light or spirit because your energy and vibrancy are contagious. I thank God for being your son.

PREFACE

As I continue to grow and learn, I am constantly reminded that everything I go through, be it pleasant or not so pleasant, all boils down to perception. I challenge you to explore different perceptions as opposed to one-sided viewpoints that may have been branded on your mind. Often, in order to tap into YOUR destiny, you must be willing to go against the grain and do something different. Understand those two words, "Your Destiny"! Not my destiny, not your parents' destiny, not your siblings' destiny, not your friends' destiny—Your Destiny! Too often we fail to understand that we are unique and different, resulting in our spending most of our lives doing the best we can to become carbon copies.

INTRODUCTION: WHO IS JAY WHITE?

I was born Jerry Lee White, Jr. on January 6, 1973 to Carolyn and Jerry White in Cincinnati, Ohio. I have two sisters by my biological parents (Yvonne and Linia) and two half-sisters and a brother by my father (Terry, Donnie, and Yvette). My parents divorced when I was a child, leaving my two sisters and me with my mother. This is not to say that my father didn't love us, but it does mean that there were voids in our lives from his not being there. Sure, he'd spend time with us on the weekends, even take us on trips around the country, but his absence in the home on a daily basis was crucial.

I remember the times when I wished I had my father in my home, but I was too young to understand how his absence would affect my adult life. I searched for my own path because I didn't have a father to validate me. I now know that EVERY son needs a father. It is the same, I think, for daughters. Otherwise we seek validation outside the home. Some turn to gangs; others turn inward. But we all turn somewhere.

I was blessed to have someone in my life that not only validated me but also changed me forever. His name was Cassanova White, Jr., and he was my cousin, the son of my father's brother. We called him Gabby because he truly had the gift of gab. Everybody loved Gabby because he could make you laugh all day. Six years older than I, Gabby taught me significant things that I needed to know for where I was in my life. He and I became close when I was just a sophomore in high school. When he sent me shoes and sweatshirts from the college he attended, I wore them proudly. Especially when I stepped inside the doors of my high school. Everyone would always ask where I got my shoes because the colors would always be exotic. I'd always tell them that I got them from my cousin Gabby.

Besides being my cousin, Gabby was my hero. He taught me about females and how to treat a lady. He taught me about money and how to make it legitimately by buying products low and marking them up for a profit. He taught me about street life and how to stay away from the wrong crowds. He taught me about independence and what it meant to be a young man who could ultimately stand on his own two feet. These were and still are valuable life lessons. However, the most important thing Gabby ever taught me was how much control I could not and would not ever have over my path in life. We'll revisit that point a bit later.

My high school years marked the beginning of my popularity, not only in my small suburban community but throughout Cincinnati. Blessed with the gift of cutting hair, I was considered a "master fader" because I could give a five-minute haircut with any design imaginable. The word about my skills as a barber quickly spread. It all began one day when my mother (my barber by default) was too tired to give me a haircut. I somehow got up the nerve to cut it myself, thinking that if anybody was going to mess up my hair, then it would be me. In my opinion, I never did.

Subsequently, my neighbor Kenrick became my guinea pig. Not only would he allow me to give him a haircut, but he also permitted me to experiment by cutting different designs in his head. I carved everything from logos such as Nike signs to people and characters such as Malcolm X and Bart Simpson. Once I had mastered the designs, people began to line up outside my door as though I were giving away money. Even white guys traveled to my house from other parts of the city to get haircuts, and yes, they too would get designs. My barbering skills gave me options because I now had money in my pocket. This gift later enabled me to move to Los Angeles, where I resided for over six years, and then to Atlanta, which I now call home.

After graduating from Greenhills High School, I attended Urbana University. This happened after a yearlong bout I had with the state of Ohio for being kicked out of Wilmington College on charges of complicity in drug trafficking. It didn't matter that during the course of my trial I was offered a full scholarship to attend Wilberforce College in Wilberforce Ohio, I was not permitted to attend any college in the country because I had a drug case pending. It is important to note that I never sold a drug in my life; however I did know some people who did. Not only did I know them, but I also played on the same basketball team as they did. Eventually I was exonerated, but the case was a major turning point in my life.

In order for you to tap into your destiny, there will come a time in your life when you have to let some people go. It might be teachers, peers you met along the way, someone you're dating, or even family members. You will have to go through a period of isolation in order to realize your destiny. For some it means being shipped off to jail; for others it may involve going off to college or joining the military. While you're in the land of the living, only one thing is certain—the fact that one day you will die alone. You came into this world by yourself, and that's how you're leaving.

Urbana was good for me in a number of ways. I made life-long friends, received a partial athletic scholarship to play basketball, excelled in academics, and was even inducted into the Urbana University Hall of Fame ten short years after I graduated. However, the most important thing I learned during my college experience was the ability to "hustle." Even though my mother endorsed going to college and whole-heartedly felt like college was the key that would unlock all of the closed doors here in America, college taught me nothing academically that I didn't already know. They called it buying low and selling high, but I merely called it simply hustling!

For me, hustling denotes the ability to take a product or service and exchange it for money or resources that are beneficial to my goals at the time. College merely taught me the so-called proper terminology for applying this fundamental drive in managing one's life. **I'm not saying that I wish I would've done something different, but I am suggesting that had it not been for the love of basketball, there's a good chance that I never would've attended college in the first place.**

Throughout this book, I should interject here, I will make references to being a filmmaker. One of the things I didn't have to learn but knew right away was that, although I had read about Spike Lee, John Singleton, Rusty Cundiff, Casey Lemon, and Robert Townsend, I could not be any of them. Nor did I want to! They are the best at being themselves. I'm the best at being Jay, and you are the best at being you. I often had to correct people who would say, "You're going to be the next Tyler Perry," or "You're the next Spike Lee." I'm neither. I'm Jay, and you're YOU—fearfully and wonderfully made, a unique creation of God.

Returning to my narrative, after graduating from Urbana I played basketball for a few months overseas with an organization called Athletes in Action. The experience was good for me because it made possible my first international trip. I traveled to Sweden, Poland, Denmark, and Germany. This too was a life-changing event because just before graduating from Urbana I received a letter from sports agent Petri Rosenquest, who lived in Sodertalja, Sweden, requesting game footage in an effort to sign me as a professional basketball player in his country.

I don't know how he got my address or obtained statistics that would make him take an interest in me. After all, Urbana is a small NAIA (National Association of Intercollegiate Athletics) school with fewer than 2,000 students. This had to be the big break I was looking for because Sweden was one of the countries that Athletes in Action was scheduled to tour. I was going to compete right in the backyard of a guy who had sought me out to play basketball professionally. When I told Mr. Rosenquest that I would be coming to his city, he grew more eager for my arrival.

Once our team arrived in Europe, we had a game in Poland where we played against some of the strongest competition I'd ever faced. Not only were the guys bigger than most college players in my division, but they could also shoot well. One advantage we had over them, however, was quickness. I went around those guarding me as though they weren't even there. I especially remember one game in which a seven-footer tried to catch me on a fast break and block my dunk.

Not only did I dunk over his outstretched hands, but after I let go of the rim the crowd went bananas. I thought to myself, "If only Petri Rosenquest were here for this, I'd be signing a contract after the game." I went on to put up decent numbers but didn't get a chance to play the minutes I was accustomed to in college because Athletes in Action was an organization that wanted all the team members to get equal playing time. This was not a problem; I just had to put up big numbers when we played in Sodertalja.

19

Game day finally arrived and it was time for me to do my thing. The stage had been set; there was no turning back. I didn't get a chance to meet Mr. Rosenquest before the game, but I was certain that he was there watching with other scouts. I wouldn't have known him if he were sitting on the bench with us because our only exchange had been a letter and a couple of phone conversations. The game began. Only a few short moments had passed before I scored my first basket, a slam-dunk from the baseline. The crowd went ballistic. I felt myself making my dreams come true until . . . .

The next few minutes of the game changed the course of my life forever. No, I didn't get hurt or embroiled in a fight. Instead, I got in foul trouble. Right after I dunked the basketball, the referees whistled me for three quick fouls. Throughout my entire college career of playing the game I can count on one hand the number of times I've fouled out. I couldn't believe it. Was this some type of vendetta the referees had against me because I had dunked the basketball? Or was it because the home fans cheered as a result? Time continued to tick away on the game clock, and so did my opportunity. I never sat on a bench for so long in my entire life. I don't even remember playing in the second half of the game.

As far as my opportunity to play professionally was concerned, Petri left me a note on a yellow piece of paper delivered by the coach that read: "Jerry, sorry for the unfortunate turn of events in this game, but I don't think you're ready for our team."

I'll admit that I had an attitude for the rest of the overseas trip. Was it a coincidence that I got into foul trouble on the biggest stage of my life so far? Knowing what I know now, I say absolutely not. That whole situation was designed to teach me that God is in control and that He had a different path for me.

The other facet of what Athletes in Action does is to prepare its participants to speak in front of people. We used basketball as bait to draw in thousands of people, then during the halftime of our games we would share our individual testimonies about what we knew about Jesus personally in an effort to win souls for the Lord. The entire experience with Athletes in Action was nothing more than a prelude for God to prepare me for where He was taking me.

You must understand by now that there is nothing more important than knowing our Creator.

Although it would take me years later to comprehend, I now can look back and see clearly how God used that whole situation as a tool of spiritual preparation. Everything from my college selection to playing over seas with Athletes in Action was nothing more than a set up.

As you tap into your destiny, be mindful of similar patterns in your life. Even when you experience disappointment, do your best to interpret the situation properly. Yes, it was an embarrassing time for me. Yes, I felt as if I had failed on the biggest stage of my life. I now look upon the episode as a small piece in this huge puzzle of life. What you do with your situation will determine where you go from there and how fast you arrive. A good friend of mine who lives in Los Angeles often remarks, "It's not what happens to you that counts. It's what you *think* about what happens to you."

23

WRITING DOWN YOUR VISION
AND BEING ABLE TO SEE IT DAILY

During a visit to my friends' house in California, I found their short and long-term goals written in dry-erase marker on the bathroom mirror. There were paragraphs upon paragraphs of their goals and a timeline for fulfilling them. Although I never wrote my goals down on the mirror, the practice taught me something about being able to see daily what you are seeking to achieve. Not a day passes that my friends aren't reminded of why they are hustling, doing what they need to do to get the results they desire.

Habbakuk 2:2 "Then the Lord answered me and said, record the vision and inscribe it on tablets, that the one who reads it may run. For the vision is yet for the appointed time; it hastens toward the goal and it will not fail though it tarries, wait for it; for it will certainly come, it will not delay."

My goals hang on the wall; they are on my computer; they are on my phone; they are in my car. No matter where I turn, I see something relevant to my vision. Not only do I see it, but my closest counterparts see it as well. It's important for them to see it so that they can keep me accountable. Habbakuk 2:2 (New America Standard Bible) states, "Then the Lord answered me and said, record the vision and inscribe it on tablets, that the one who reads it may run. For the vision is yet for the appointed time; it hastens toward the goal and it will not fail though it tarries, wait for it; for it will certainly come, it will not delay." In other words, your vision should be so clear that anyone should be able to see it as a plan for action.

It doesn't matter if you are a gifted writer or not. My penmanship is horrible, but I scribble notes to myself or load them onto my phone. You must find a way to get your ideas from your head to something tangible that you can see every day. If you can't see it, you need to be able to hear it. If you can't hear it, you need to be able to smell it. If you can't smell it, you need to be able to touch it. It ought to make you stub your toe in the morning. It ought to make you restless and anxious to get at it. It ought to make you bored and unfulfilled when you're not around it. Your friends ought to get tired of hearing about it. You should be thinking about it when you're not hustling, working a job, or going to school.

When we are not able to see our goals daily, we allow opportunities to escape. If we don't make decisions that will change our lives, life itself will go on and make us fit in. Too often we fail ourselves because we allow life's inexorable flow to dictate the terms.

When we are not able to see our goals daily, we allow opportunities to escape.

LOVE THYSELF

I believe that our parents or guardians are the most influential people in our lives while we are being reared up. They can be the best thing that ever happened to us but unfortunately they can be the worst thing that ever happened to us - not only our parents but our peers alike. We tend to allow parents and peers to dictate where we should be in our lives by a certain age, and if we're not there then we may allow ourselves to be labeled as failures or fools.

If we embrace these labels or other non-edifying titles used to describe us, it could lead us on a downward spiral because we haven't taken the time to love our self. We do so many things trying to accommodate for self-love not realizing that there is no substitute externally for what has to be realized internally. Self-love starts within, not without!

The right person can say the right thing to us and we melt in submission, taking their word(s) as the gospel. However, the right person can say the wrong thing about us and our day is shattered.

For example: You can have on the nicest outfit with all of the accessories to match, but if you don't receive a compliment from the person/people **you choose** to

27

validate you, your day is ruined. It doesn't matter if the world acknowledges that your outfit is wonderful, if the right people don't say so, it is often a blow to our self-esteem, making us question our value. This type of bruise potentially causes a chain of unhealthy living that looks something like this.

We don't get the approval we are seeking from the individual(s). In the process of trying to gain approval, we subscribe to the latest fashions and other material in an effort to "win" attention. In search of a compliment from that special someone, we create financial obligations for ourselves, even though they have no real significance as it pertains to *our Destiny*. When we create financial obligations for ourselves, it requires us to get a JOB to keep up with life. There is nothing wrong with using a job as a steppingstone to advance us to the next level, but we often aren't going to the next level because we are simply *surviving* - trying to support a lifestyle that *we* created. Then we find ourselves unhappy in a situation that we created, so we seek happiness and fulfillment from other people. Most often, it's looking for a man or woman to fill the void that only achievement of *our Destiny* can fulfill. I'm not saying that companionship is a bad thing.

As a matter of fact I think it's a great thing, but not if it becomes a substitute for self-love. The problem that many of us have however; is that we look to another individual to be our end all be all. This results from leading with our flesh.

I'll take it a step further. We sometimes misinterpret why a person is in our lives during a season (some more critical than others), especially when there's an attraction. This in many cases leads us across boundaries that we should not venture across. It's called SEX!

There is nothing wrong with using a job as a steppingstone to advance us to the next level, but we often aren't going to the next level because we are simply surviving - trying to support bills or habits that we created.

I wonder how many of us have destroyed relationships that "could've been great" because we had sex with the individual. I wonder how many of us have overlooked possibilities of who the person we're "attracted" to could've introduced us to, had we not crossed the SEX line: a business relationship, a prayer partner, a mate?

Once the companionship that should be strictly Platonic is laced with sex, it further puts us away from our destiny because we have opened up a can of feel good which we most often times aren't able to control.

Then the person walks away from us. It's okay to move on. What's not okay is for us to become so dependent on the other person to provide us with happiness and fulfillment that when he or she leaves, they take our "stuff" with them.

Rather than preparing ourselves for a mate or partner that can help us get to our destiny, we tend to lead with our flesh and make decisions that get us off the path. Whether we are seeking a mate, compliments from our peers or someone to tell us we're doing a good job, we should love ourselves enough first to the point where we are fulfilled if those words of affirmation are given or not.

This is why it is imperative to ask God to give us knowledge of self and revelation of how HE feels about us. Immediately following this, I believe we should ask God to order our steps and guide us to the people we need, not just the people we want. This is a good time to tell you that God already knows the ending of your story, so wouldn't it make sense to consult Him about the chapters?

I wonder how many of us have destroyed relationships that "could've been great" because we had sex with the individual.

THE LAND OF MILK AND HONEY

Numbers 13:1-20 recounts how God commanded Moses to send spies to the land of Canaan to search it out. Moses then picked twelve leaders, one leader from each tribe, to carry out the mandate of discovering a land of milk and honey.

Not everyone, of course, has the resources to search out a land of milk and honey through actual travel. However, there is a viable alternative—the World Wide Web. The web will take you anywhere in the world you want to go, but you have to undertake the research.

I will never forget residing in Cincinnati on 17 January 1998 and within a twenty-four-hour period spontaneously moving to Los Angeles. I knew that Cincinnati, and the state of Ohio for that matter, was entirely too small as an arena for realizing my dreams. I wanted to pursue acting and modeling; therefore, I was headed to either New York or California. Much like the biblical spies, I was fortunate enough to be able to scout the land before I moved there. I knew beyond a shadow of a doubt that one of those places would be my domain because it represented milk and honey. Though I didn't pray before I moved, God intervened anyway. Just when

I had made up my mind to leave Cincinnati, my stepfather Tony called to say that he was ready to leave Los Angeles and move back to Ohio. He and my mother had been living apart temporarily while he cared for an ailing relative in California. The news of his return was fortunate because I was able to live in his Los Angeles house practically rent-free. Although I left behind everything and everybody I knew to head for the city of angels, there was never a time that I was fearful.

Having faith in God enabled me to live free of stress and worry in Watts at 103rd and Avalon. I lived amid Crips, Bloods, and crooked cops, but at no time did I ever have any trepidation. It didn't matter that I had no family or loved ones to come home to. The only thing that mattered was the fact that I had the courage to pursue my dreams.

Los Angeles blew my mind. I couldn't believe how many businesses there were in the "hood" and how they were all interconnected. Needless to say, it wasn't like that in Cincinnati. I saw black people and Latinos everywhere I turned, and for the most part everybody got along fine. My neighbors to the left of me were black, and my neighbors to the right were Latinos.

I didn't have clusters of grapes as did the biblical spies, but I did have a huge cactus in my front yard, Calla lilies, Birds of Paradise, and heaps of roses. In the backyard were a lemon tree, peach tree, fig tree, and another variety that bore nuts. Although the house I lived in was very small, it was my safe haven, largely due to the recent presence of the late Minister Ideal Asuncion. Aunt Ideal's spirit and prophetic words remained with me in that house and to this very day.

In Los Angeles I got a job working in an Inglewood barbershop after only two days of living in the city of angels. Once again, my gift with the clippers paved the way for me. Of course, I had my book of designs to help sell my skills, even without a barber's license. The only explanation that I have for being able to work without a license was God's favor. Wherever I went people never gave me a problem, until the day when the owner of the barbershop I worked in became jealous.

Now that I think about it, he probably always was jealous of me. I was confident and courteous - qualities that made me different in that context. I went out of my way to help people and many times gave without the expectation of receiving. I guess that was what antagonized my boss at the time.

LEARNING THE VALUE OF INCONVENIENCE

Here I should address two situations that complicated my daily existence in Los Angeles. The first is that during early 1998 the city was experiencing a storm called "El Nino," which caused it to rain non-stop, triggering widespread flooding, landslides, and automobile accidents. El Nino thus made a liar out of the song "It Never Rains in Southern California" and altered my expectations of this land of milk and honey.

El Nino was the first inconvenience that I encountered, largely due to the fact that I didn't own a vehicle at the time. As a result, the second inconvenience was that I had to ride the bus to and from work every day. The good thing about this second situation was that my bus dropped me off right in front of my house and, after a transfer, dropped me off right in front of the barbershop. Do you see how I had to be focused? There was no room or reason for me to deviate off of the path. If I wanted to participate in anything extracurricular, it would come with another layer of inconvenience.

Tapping into your destiny requires a bit of discomfort to develop a level of independence. It's good to be hungry sometimes and to have only limited options. I

35

never had to depend on public transportation until I moved to Los Angeles because I always had a car or someone to take me where I needed to go, but there are some points in life where we have to learn how to become independent—even when it means swallowing our pride and doing something that we never pictured ourselves doing in order to make ends meet. For some of us it's bussing tables at a local restaurant, while for others it may be skateboarding to your destination. It also may mean that you have to flip burgers at a hamburger joint. Whatever your case may be, at some point you are going to have to show a degree of humility in order to get the job done. This phase in your life, which I call "Learning the Value of Inconvenience," is necessary for a deeper understanding of sacrifice for the sake of realizing your goals.

Tapping into your destiny requires a bit of discomfort to develop a level of independence. It's good to be hungry sometimes and to have only limited options.

CREATE OPPORTUNITY

There is a story in the Bible that I feel the need to reference because it is relevant to this life-changing phase in my life. Maybe you've had or will have a similar experience. The source is 2 Kings 7:3-8:

> Now there were four leprous men at the entrance of the gate; and they said to one another, "Why do we sit here until we die? If we say we will enter the city, then the famine is in the city and we will die there; and if we sit here, we die also. Now therefore come, and let us go over to the camp of the Arameans. If they spare us, we will live; and if they kill us, we will but die." They arose at *twilight* to go to the camp of the Arameans; when they came to the outskirts of the camp of the Arameans, behold, there was no one there. For the Lord had caused the army of the Arameans to hear a sound of chariots and a sound of horses, even the sound of a great army, so that they said to one another, "Behold, the king of Israel has hired against us the kings of the Hittites and the kings of the Egyptians to come upon us." Therefore they arose and fled in the *twilight*, and left their tents and their horses and their

donkeys, even the camp as it was, and fled for their life. When these lepers came to the outskirts of the camp, they entered one tent and ate and drank, and carried from there silver and gold and clothes, and went and hid them; and they returned and entered another tent and carried from there also, and went and hid them.

Business was slow for everyone in the shop except the owner, and I couldn't understand how the other barbers could just sit there and starve. Day after day I witnessed each barber sitting on the edge of his chair for a full day without cutting a single head. They were like chained animals.

Much like the four lepers, I just couldn't sit there and starve to death. I knew that, if I waited for an opportunity to come to me, not only would I starve financially but also I would prove everyone who was against me right. Instead, I took it upon myself to get some flyers made and hit the streets. My bait was a half-page circular that read, "FREE HAIRCUT," in the center followed by the fine-print announcement, "If you're not satisfied." Once I got customers' attention, the rest was history.

All I needed was an opportunity. However, opportunity means nothing without action. The lepers were willing to take action and once they made up their minds, something miraculous happened. If you take a close look, you'll notice that it was *at twilight* when the lepers made up their minds and acted. The same time that the lepers made up their minds coincides with when God caused the Arameans to hear the sound of chariots and horses to the point where they were afraid and fled. God is bigger than any giant you may have to face. God honored the lepers' faith and worked to reward them. Not when they got to their destination, but the moment they took a step of faith, God stepped in and did His thing. What opportunity are you willing to create for yourself?

> *Much like the four lepers, I just couldn't sit there and starve to death. I knew that, if I waited for an opportunity to come to me, not only would I starve financially but also I would prove everyone who was against me right.*

For me it was making up my mind to play offense instead of defense. Because I did this day in and day out, my clientele grew vastly over the first eight months of my living in Los Angeles. Little did I know that I would need every person I managed to reel in because of a stunt by the owner that made me pack my bags and leave the shop before a physical altercation broke out.

COMPETITION IN THE LAND

Nothing is more important in your life than your destiny. As the author and finisher of our faith (Hebrews 12:2), God has preordained our lives. Fulfillment of your destiny, however, won't come without trials. You must understand that if there is something good to be had, you are not the only one who wants it. Yes, it may be your destiny, but many people are ready to usurp or imitate it. Take the music industry, for example. There is nothing wrong with being an entertainer, but there is something terribly wrong with trying to be identical to someone else and forsaking one's own identity.

Let's consider the spies again. Notice that God sent them specifically to *spy* out the land. At this particular time God didn't tell them to possess the land. He told them to spy—to discover something by close observation. Why? Because people were already there occupying the space. If no one had occupied the land, the spies wouldn't have needed to go. When the spies came back with their report, they knew the type of people who were there. They knew how strong the city was. They even knew the different types of people by tribe. In other words, they did their research.

Don't be naïve and think that there aren't people in your spot. Tapping into your destiny will mean doing your homework to find out the steps you need to take to occupy your land of milk and honey.

You must understand that if there is something good to be had, you are not the only one who wants it.

FORCED OUT

Situations will occur throughout our lives to push us from one season into the next. One of my mentors remarked, "In order for some things to begin, other things must come to an end. In order for some things to live, some things must die." I have found both statements to be true. Think about it. In order for high school to begin, middle school must come to an end. In order for a marriage to begin, bachelorhood must come to an end. In order for spring to begin, winter must come to an end. The point I'm making is that seasons change in our lives.

Many times they change without our permission, and it has to be this way because in order to tap into our destiny we may need to be forced out. Why? Because of fear or comfort. I have witnessed many situations where people close to me were forced out. Take my friend Terence for instance. Terence is an author, poet and motivational speaker that was recently fired from a job he despised. Now Terence has committed 100% of his time focusing on his passion and purpose – speaking and changing lives.

Shannon is another close friend that was recently forced out. She was married to her spouse for five years when all of a sudden, he decided that he no longer wanted to be married to her. This sudden change of heart on his behalf forced Shannon out of "their" home and into her own. It forced her to stand on her own two feet rather than depending on him to provide for her and their children. Although this case is a bit extreme, some aspects of life has a way of forcing us out of our comfort zone and one step closer to our destiny.

> *"In order for some things to begin, other things must come to an end. In order for some things to live, some things must die."*

I didn't know until the morning of 1 August 1998 that God had a plan to push me into the next season of my life.

One day I had the pleasure of cutting the hair of a client named Lisa. She wore her hair short and curly because she was big on fitness and an avid trainer, so she didn't want to worry about high maintenance of her hair after workouts. After I gave her a haircut, she didn't have anything except large-denomination bills, and nobody in the shop had change. I thus went to the store a few doors down to get change for her. When I returned, she was standing outside the barbershop crying. I couldn't imagine what had happened because I'd been gone for only a few minutes.

It turned out that Emmanuel, the owner of the shop, had sexually insulted Lisa. Never before in my life had I snapped so abruptly. It was as though someone had humiliated my mother. Rather than beating the old fellow as I was tempted to do, I just packed my belongings and headed for the door. On my way out he had the nerve to ask me, "Are you going to take your clients with you?" (Subconsciously I had known that this day would come, so I had been preparing for it by recording my clients' contact information.) I was so furious that I couldn't stand at the bus stop directly in front of the barbershop but walked half a mile to the next one to cool off.

Then it happened. As I was walking, not thinking clearly because I had just left my place of employment without having another job, I met a Jewish man named Tim Munyer. Tim was cleaning out a storefront to get it ready for a new tenant. As it happened, the storefront used to be a barbershop/beauty salon. As I was passing the window, he was putting up a "For Rent" sign. I stopped in disbelief as he locked the doors. "Wait a minute, sir," I said. "How much do you want for the place?" Mr. Munyer reopened the door and gave me a brief history of the facility, in particular its previous tenants. The history was irrelevant to me, but what stood

46

out in my mind then as now was Tim's comment about not living in Los Angeles but only being there to get this particular piece of property ready for occupancy.

Little did I know when I woke up that morning, I would be walking out of an old season of my life into a new and ordained one. I literally walked from a stumbling block into a steppingstone. It didn't matter that in my own shop I was the only barber. It didn't matter how I was going to pay the $650 monthly rent. It didn't matter that I lacked a chair, sink, or dryer. It didn't matter that I was without a barber's license. The only thing that mattered was that, after I signed the lease the next day, everything I needed to move forward and be effective was provided for me.

One of the girls with whom I worked had some stylist chairs at her house that she sold me for almost nothing. I still didn't have a car, but one day a good friend of mine picked me up from work and took me home. On the way there we stopped by a garage sale where I ended up buying two black leather sofas for a total of $400. I was extremely blessed. The same week I met a gentleman who was in the business of commercial signage. He gave me a break and put signs on my store's window for a modest fee. I named the business "Gabby's Place" in remembrance of my cousin and hero.

Little did I know when I woke up that morning, I would be walking out of an old season of my life into a new and ordained one.

NECESSARY CASUALTIES

This is an appropriate place to talk about Gabby because you have to understand that tapping into your destiny means that at some point in your life you need to release control of certain elements. Yes, it may seem elementary, but there are some people, places, and things you will need to leave behind.

On 22 December 1992, a cold day in Cincinnati, Gabby and I were stranded at his mother's house on Hawkhurst Lane. We sat in his mother's kitchen eating Fruity Pebbles at about 6:00 p.m., and it had grown dark outside. I remember Gabby asking his sister Carmen, or "Lady" as we called her, for permission to use her silver Toyota and being denied. His mother also declined a request to borrow her burgundy Nissan.

I don't ever remember a time in my life where I've ever been stranded. Him either! Gabby and I were both popular and liked by most people in the city (as far as we know) and this had never before happened. On that night in particular, I remember hearing a voice inside saying, "Do not go to the gym!" What is unclear to me now, as it was then, is the question of whether God was warning me, or if I was imagining it. We were either so desperate to play the game of basketball or to prideful to accept the fact that two socially popular people were stuck. In any event, somebody picked us up, and we headed out to the gym to play basketball anyway. We hadn't been in the gym ten minutes when the most bizarre, catastrophic, and life-changing event of my life took place.

Gabby and I were chosen for the same team. On the first play I passed the ball to Gabby, who immediately took what would be the first shot of the game, and the last shot of his life. I remember his missing the shot and the other team running a fast break to the other end of the court. Gabby, on the other hand, walked three or four short paces toward the baseline and then abruptly sat down on the floor with his arms around his knees. Gabby was always a natural jokester. From the far end of the court I watched him lie back and put his hands behind his head as though he were taking a nap. Several of us blurted out, "Quit playing." What we didn't realize, Gabby wasn't joking this time. He was having a seizure.

I remember him lying back on the floor with his arms outstretched. His tongue was lashing from side to side, and his eyes were rolling back in his head. Then, a few moments later, Gabby began to snore hoarsely, as though he had fallen into a deep sleep. I tried to wake him up, but there was no response. Within a few seconds he stopped breathing. I immediately fell to my knees, climbed on top of him, and began mouth-to-mouth resuscitation. One of the older guys in charge of the gym pulled me back, stating that we should give Gabby some room. I obeyed out of shock, deferring to a man a lot older and wiser. Now and again I wonder if I made a mistake by stopping the resuscitation process, but I am comforted in knowing that it was just Gabby's time to go home.

It took the paramedics over twenty minutes to arrive, though it should have taken no more than five given their location just around the corner. Someone from the gym drove me to the hospital. When I got there, they had already pronounced Gabby dead. I remember seeing him lying on a table with a tag on his big toe. My hero was dead.

At Gabby's funeral I cursed God the whole time, wondering how He could take such a good person away from me. Jesus had a similar experience the day when Lazarus died. The news was so devastating that Jesus didn't move for two whole days. I strongly believe that Jesus' devastation stemmed from his grief and concern for Mary and Martha, Lazarus' sisters.

In John 11:21 Martha said to Jesus, "'Lord, if thou had been here, my brother had not died.'"

In verse 32 Mary repeats those same words. What Martha and Mary later discovered, however, was that Lazarus' death brought about greater faith. Shortly after Gabby's death, I realized that I would never have the power to prolong life. Neither will you.

Some years later I came to understand why God took Gabby away from me. My interpretation is that God will not allow us to put anyone or anything before Him. Furthermore, while tapping into your ordained destiny, casualties and losses in life are inevitable. This is so, not because people necessarily *deserve* to die but because they cannot become what only God can be for us. This doesn't mean that a person has to literally die in order to become a casualty in your life. Some people you will have to delete from your phone, erase from your email database, change your telephone number or even change addresses.

You cannot realize your destiny by living your life for other people. You must pursue what God has arranged for you. We often have big dreams and goals that are shaped by the influence of people we choose to validate us. As a result of Gabby's death I was forced to live MY purpose and not his. Take the time to observe the casualties in your life and assess what lesson they served to impart. Seasons change and casualties are necessary for you to tap into your destiny.

You cannot realize your destiny by living your life for other people. You must pursue what God has arranged for you.

THE DASH

If you haven't gained inspiration by now, let me take a more harsher/realistic approach – it all boils down to your interpretation. No matter how healthy you eat, how much money you have, how many degrees you hold, whether you believe in a higher power or not, how many times you go to the gym or who you know in high places, one day you will die and so will I. Yes we tend to hope that it's later on in life as opposed to sooner, but dying is inevitable. Not even a mother's love can keep you around forever.

Since this is a reality that no one can escape, I'd like to spend a few moments and talk about the *dash*. I have collected quite a few obituaries throughout my life and one thing they all have in common is the *dash*. The dash is the hyphen between the date of birth and the date of death. If you haven't attended a funeral or seen an obituary before, it looks something like this: Sunrise July 5, 1852 – Sunset October 31, 1912. The dash represents what that particular individual did with their life while they were living. We can all recollect when we came into the world, but none of us know exactly when we'll die, that is, unless for some unfortunate reason we plan it.

Although we may not know all of the details of a person's life, God does. What we do know however, is who the particular individual was to us. If they were kind to us, nine times out of ten, that is how we would remember them. If they were not so pleasant to us, that's probably what we'll remember the most about them. The same is true if we were encouraged or discouraged by the individual.

I've been to funerals where people went up to the podium and spoke highly of people and I've been to funerals when people flat out lied about how good of a person the deceased had been.

I remember attending a funeral for a gentleman a few years back when nobody really wanted to take the microphone to say something good on behalf of the deceased. At least if they did they didn't show it or voice it. It was so bad that the pastor had to stand in the gap and shift the topic by making a joke.

Here's a question. If you were to die today, who would come to your funeral and what would they say?

I believe that we are going to inspire people one way or the other. Either our lives will be viewed as an example of what possibilities exist, or it will be a testament of how not to live. The reason. Self-fulfillment!

Take a moment and think about someone who has inspired you in a way that changed your life. It can be for the good or the not so good. We are all products of our environment. If our environment was filled with love and support, there's a good chance that we will reflect that throughout our day. Likewise, if we are products of a not so positive environment, chances are that's what we'll reflect.

It is this theory that leads me to believe, each one of us constantly pours into the people that we come into contact with. For example: do you know of anyone that automatically goes negative when an idea is presented? Maybe you and a group of your friends decide that you want to go to one place, but this particular individual always presents a confrontation. They can't ever just go with the flow and an argument always manifests. We all have our moments, but what happens when this type of behavior always occurs with this particular person? It's so evident, that you can predict the outcome of the conversation. Is it a good chance that this person grew up in an environment where confrontation was a regular? When we are in our destiny, I believe that we exude peace and fulfillment that inevitably becomes contagious.

Recently, there have been celebrities in the news reporting their death. There is one celebrity in particular that I want to give remarks about because of his dash.

Michael Jackson (anointed "The King of Pop") died and brought the entire world to a standstill if but for a moment. The news covered reactions of his fans throughout the world about the loss of such a phenomenal entertainer. There were Michael Jackson t-shirts and memorabilia sold everywhere from street corners to gas stations. There were street performers, aspiring entertainers and average everyday people doing their impersonation of Michael Jackson all over the world.

There is even a famous Youtube video being viewed all around the globe of a group of incarcerated men that came together in their facility and made up a routine resembling the "Thriller" video as a tribute to the late king of pop, Michael Jackson.

Although many people feel like Michael Jackson's death happened way to soon, there is no mistake that Jackson left an indelible impression on the world and had an incredible dash. Personally, I believe that everyone born between 1960 and 1985 at least made one attempt to do the "moonwalk" (a dance that Michael Jackson created and made him famous).

Michael's dash may be a bit extreme, but there are people we walk by and have encounters with every single day that have incredible dashes. They don't have perfect lives but they have taken chances and walk in their destiny. You can recognize them fairly easy because they are the people who love going to work everyday or what they do. They are the people who always have a smile on their face and have nothing but positive words to say. They are the people who have goals and dreams and are in pursuit of them everyday. Finally, they are the people who are not envious or jealous of other people that are succeeding.

My questions for you are simple: What are you doing with your life? Are you afraid of losing "stuff" or giving some things back? Do you need "stuff" to make you happy and fulfilled? Do your material possessions define you? Are you bound by other peoples' opinion of you and what you should do or should not do?

When was the last time you took a real vacation? When was the last time you visited that special person? Have you truly forgiven that person who hurt you? When was the last time you took yourself out to dinner or a movie and enjoyed your own company? Have you truly faced your greatest fear(s)? The best part of your life is in front of you if you take the step! What is going on in your dash?

If you were to die today, who would come to your funeral and what would they say?

DISCIPLINE

Once you have been exposed to adversity, you are better equipped to make decisions about your life's direction. In many cases you will discover your destiny, by which I mean something about which you are passionate. A wise woman once told me that, whenever you find your passion, it's at that point that you won't need someone to micromanage you because you'll eat it, sleep it, think it, and be it. However, there comes a point in this discovery process where you will have to exercise the discipline it takes to master the gift. You may need to attend school to learn more or do more research in the library. For me it happened a few different times. First, it was filmmaking.

I will never forget the time when I moved into my first barbershop. I spent countless hours in the shop alone. As I sat there, God began to encourage me to write about my life in order to help other people overcome their past and discover their destiny. At the time I didn't necessarily understand the prompting, but eventually it would all make sense.

Sitting on the black leather sofa, I began to write my ideas down on notebook paper in red ink. I would sit there for hours and just write. It started out as one long story that resembled a book report, and I soon had over a hundred pages of anecdotes from my journey. Whenever I got a break from a client, I sat on the couch and wrote. Then one of the most significant persons in my life showed up.

Once you have been exposed to adversity, you are better equipped to make decisions about your life's direction.

Robert Fletcher was a client who would stop by from time to time to see me even when he wasn't getting a haircut. One day, seeing me composing page after page, Robert asked what I was writing. I told him that it was something about "my life growing up in Cincinnati." When I read a few of the stories that I had written, he stated that I should turn some of them into a movie. Although I agreed, I didn't take his comment seriously.

He departed only to return the following day with a book about writing scripts. It was a relatively thin book that explained how to put a narrative into script form.

Guided by the manual, I began to arrange my ideas in script form with characters in the proper format. He later brought me another book titled *African American Screenwriters Now*, which was a compilation of short stories about black filmmakers. Reading this book opened my eyes to the possibility of becoming a filmmaker. It was at this point that I began to research the profession. Robert had exposed me to a world that I had no idea I could conquer, and I am grateful to him for seeing something in me that I had not glimpsed.

The point I'm making is that, when Robert exposed me to the possibility of writing scripts, I followed up on the idea. I had grown up watching movies, but never had I imagined writing them. Maybe I didn't think my stories were interesting or relevant. In any event, Robert had exposed me to something different that I loved. I went to bed writing, and I woke up writing. It was like giving a painter his first set of brushes and an easel.

At this early time I was running on pure adrenaline and therefore didn't need discipline. That part came later when I had writer's block or when I wanted to party rather than stay home and work. To this day I still have to challenge myself at times to write when I don't necessarily feel like doing so.

You are going to have to make up your mind to take your gift to the next level by being disciplined enough to put in apprenticeship time. In the movie *The Great Debaters*, when Forest Whitaker and his son are discussing homework, the son remarks, "We do what we HAVE to do, so we can do what we WANT to do." In essence he was admitting that he needed to sacrifice now in order to be free later. You and I are no different. We must invest the time that it will take to perfect our gifts.

Maybe I didn't think my stories were interesting or relevant. "I hope you believe that you're relevant and interesting, whatever it is that you do!"

DANCING WITH THE STARS

The second area that required me to be disciplined was tap-dancing. In 2002, while living in Los Angeles, I was out on the 3rd Street Promenade one day and saw twin brothers Sean and Jon Scott tap-dancing. The Promenade is a place filled with outdoor shopping, restaurants and tourist attractions. People are there dancing, singing, doing magic tricks, martial arts and anything else that will get them discovered by Hollywood, while making money in the process. In my opinion, Sean and Jon were the exceptions. They always had a crowd around them and they were my first real experience with the skill. I'd seen Sandman on Showtime at the Apollo, but they were live and in person.

To make a long story short, we exchanged information, and I kept in touch with them. One year later I hosted an event in Watts called "One Spirit: WE'RE ALL STARS Weekend" and invited them to perform because I felt that the kids in my neighborhood needed to see these two teenagers do their thing. Little did I know that I would develop a love for tap my self.

My love for tap wouldn't take effect for another five years when I was living in Atlanta. When I found out that a local art center was offering beginner classes, my wife and I thought it would be a great way for us to spend time together as well as get some good exercise. We started taking the class, and I immediately fell in love with tap-dancing all over again, so much so that I traveled all over New York and Georgia trying to find shoes that would fit me. I wear a size 14, and it was impossible to find shoes that would fit me. I finally had to buy taps and shoes separately and have them assembled.

On 2 January 2008 I finally had a pair of tap shoes. I remember staying after class by myself in order to tap-dance longer, often staying until the art center closed. Rick Washington then would have to announce, "Time to shut it down, Happy Feet." Now I get up at 7:00 a.m. Monday through Friday to practice. I also spend a great deal of time on the Internet watching other people tap-dance in order to learn more techniques. For some people tap is a way to lose weight; for others it's a way to stay in shape. For me it's something else that I desire to conquer.

Do you need to get up at 7:00 every day to exercise your gift? If that's what it takes! Am I saying that you need to get on the Internet and spend countless hours watching other people do what you aspire to do? If that's what it takes! There will come a point when you'll have to make a decision to do what you need to do when nobody's watching. This takes discipline and focus. Once again, when you love what you do, you practice. The worst-case scenario is that friends will have to pry you away from the activity you love because it is monopolizing your time.

There will come a point when you'll have to make a decision to do what you need to do when nobody's watching.

REJECTION IS A BLESSING

Reverting to the topic of filmmaking, a key moment changed my life forever. As I stated earlier, I had the honor and privilege to write my first film and later direct it—a rare occurrence. The fact that God used me to write a movie that changed lives is nothing less than astonishing even now.

I will never forget the night when I met Magic Johnson in Los Angeles during a celebrity fashion show on Wilshire Boulevard in Beverly Hills. First, I had to sneak into the show and succeeded in doing so thanks to a client of mine named Francis, who was an official participant in the event. Francis managed to sneak me in the back door by stating that I was one of the models.

Nobody knew that I wasn't a part of the show because the place was filled with models talking, getting hair and make-up done, and just mingling. While they were busy, I found a suit on the rack that I thought would fit me and tried it on. Although the pants were a bit high around the ankles, I managed to pull it off. When Francis saw me trying on suits, he couldn't believe it.

Meeting the right person to get my film made was the only thing that mattered to me. Being in the fashion show in front of twelve hundred people only gave me more confidence to approach celebrities after the show.

Once it was over, I somehow met Magic Johnson and explained to him who I was and how he could help me produce my movie. Magic's assistant gave me a business card and asked to meet with me early the following week. I couldn't believe what was happening. First I had snuck into the fashion show as a model; then I got a chance to give my elevator speech to Magic Johnson. How could life get any better?

It is critical for you to understand that rejection is necessary and a blessing.

Before I went to the meeting, I made sure that my suit was dry-cleaned and my hair freshly trimmed. I also made sure that I arrived early and had everything ready for my big moment including a printed script, new binder, and duplicate copies. The office building itself seemed to have glass everywhere, and the landscaping was immaculate. When I got off the elevator, Magic's assistant, Sherri Sneed, met me in the lobby and took me back to an office. Once we got there, she told me that Mr. Johnson would not be available to meet with me and that she would be conducting our meeting. I didn't have time to be disappointed because I had to concentrate on accomplishing my mission.

I gave Ms. Sneed a short introduction to what the movie was about before handing over my script. It was like handing over a brand-new baby. I was careful not to drop it and made sure that she knew how important the script was to me. Everything then seemed to go in slow motion. Ms. Sneed took my script and put it on a shelf along with what seemed to be fifty other binders that looked exactly like mine. The meeting was over. Sherri stood up, shook my hand, and wished me much success, promising that they'd get back to me, but they never did.

I immediately took that as a rejection, and, even though they never actually said "You can't do it," that was how I interpreted their response. What they didn't know was that this was exactly what I needed to go to the next level. I figured that, if no one wanted to help me produce my film, then I didn't need them. I would do it myself.

Some people need cheerleaders to motivate them. I am motivated by rejection. It is critical for you to understand that rejection is necessary and a blessing. It all boils down to interpretation. Now that I have set the stage for you, let me show you how the situation prepared me for the next step in realizing my goal.

ANOTHER DIVINE APPOINTMENT

Every year that I spent away from Cincinnati where my family lived, I made it a point to visit for Thanksgiving and Christmas. It didn't matter that the holidays were a month apart. When in November 1999 I returned, I knew that I could catch up with everybody either at Golden Skates (the city skating rink) or at the notorious Ritz nightclub. On this particular trip home I visited both—Golden Skates to experiment with my handheld movie camera, and the Ritz to see old acquaintances. I had purchased a small handheld camera with the intention of shooting my movie. (You'll see on the DVD how I experimented with the camera to learn its different functions.) I remember sneaking the camera inside the skating rink and filming virtually the entire night.

At the Ritz nightclub a guy named Zarian walked up to me drinking a Corona said, "I heard you're getting ready to shoot a movie." A few things amazed me about this encounter. The first was that Zarian and I knew each other but lived in different neighborhoods and had attended different schools. Therefore, we never really had any significant interaction up to this point. The second thing that blew me away about his comment was that he was aware of my plans to shoot a movie. I don't even know whom we both knew that could have told him. I'm not one to tell a bunch of people what I'm doing anyway.

Zarian went on to tell me that he was attending what used to be Southern Ohio College in order to learn audio and video production. That statement raised my eyebrows, and I ended up going over to his house the following day for ten hours to watch him produce music. I couldn't believe his talent. When I told him about my plans, it was as though he became inspired by the vision as well.

When I returned to Cincinnati for Christmas, Zarian had inspired others with the vision. His entire class wanted to volunteer on the project. Not only did they want to volunteer, but they also were allowed use of the school's camera equipment. I went from a $300 camera to a $45,000 camera. Furthermore, Zarian's instructor, Chris Strobel, permitted us free use of every other piece of production equipment at his disposal.

I flew back to Los Angeles to begin the planning process. Before we began shooting on 18 June 2000, there was more work to be done. We had to schedule the shoot, secure locations, find props, lock in sponsors, and apply for permits, but the most important thing was to employ a cast of actors. I didn't know the first thing about securing such talent, but someone on the team did. Ms. Stella Jones Tooson not only helped secure sponsors but also persuaded the *Cincinnati Enquirer* and *Cincinnati Herald* to run casting-call advertisements. Moreover, someone I don't even know gave us free use of a five-star hotel in Springdale, Ohio. The whole time all this planning was going on, I was residing in Los Angeles.

I will never forget returning to Cincinnati in the spring of 2001 for the casting call. When I got off the airplane, I headed straight to the hotel where the auditions were going to be held. Once I got to the location, it brought tears to my eyes when I saw how God had blessed us. Inside the hotel was a line of people that stretched from the audition room all the way outside the building and around the corner—at least a hundred people waiting for an opportunity to audition for *my movie*.

Although this was one of the most unforgettable moments in my life, another was even more significant. You may be wondering what this has to do with *your* destiny. You'll soon find out.

The day before I graduated from high school, a close friend of mine was arrested for his role in an armed robbery. He was sentenced to twenty-five years in prison, the first seven being mandatory. This same friend was responsible for helping me to develop my barbering skills. Shawn was also our neighborhood fixit man. He could fix anything that was broken, from bikes to radios to hair clippers.

I hadn't seen Shawn since the day before our high-school graduation in 1991, and the first time I laid eyes on Shawn again was at the audition for my movie almost ten years later. Shawn did a good job of auditioning, but what he didn't know was that once I saw him, he already had a part in the movie. I knew that Shawn would do anything for anybody. He just had made a stupid mistake.

When I think about it, we all make stupid mistakes. Some of those mistakes warrant the need for laws while others aren't deemed as severe. Maybe Shawn's mistake was a part of his destiny.

Once I told him that he was booked for the part, he pulled me aside looking me straight in the eyes and said, "You have restored hope in my life." At that moment I realized several interconnected things. I had to encounter betrayal at the hands of peers in college, Aunt Ideal had to stay alive long enough to keep Tony at bay while God prepared me for my exodus away from my comfort zone; I had to walk out of the Cosmic Barbershop in Inglewood and into Gabby's Place; I had to meet Robert Fletcher, who gave me the books about filmmaking; I had to be rejected by Magic Johnson and his crew; I had to meet Zarian that night at the Ritz; and most importantly as it pertains to this season in my destiny, I had to produce the movie "Get Right or Get Left, which inspired so many people along the way.

Zarian Hadley subsequently moved to Los Angeles, where he now owns his own business and works on nearly every set imaginable in Hollywood.

Marcell Cunningham walked away from a hair salon in Cincinnati and also moved to Los Angeles. She got a job working in a salon called Mo'Mars, owned by the actress and comedian Monique.

Tish Norman was an aspiring actress. She and I are close friends to this day, and she is a renowned motivational speaker.

Valencia Hawkins started out as an accountant but, after working on our set, discovered that her passion was the entertainment industry. Valencia relocated to Atlanta, where she serves as Tyler Perry's personal assistant.

Michael Thompson left Cincinnati after we filmed the movie and moved to Los Angeles to pursue acting full-time.

Tapping into your destiny ultimately helps other people to tap into theirs. People need you to do what you were designed to do because the truth of the matter is that either you will need them or they will need you.

What are you waiting for?

ABOUT THE AUTHOR

Jay White has produced two independent films (*Get Right or Get Left* and *When We Were Kids*), a documentary (*I'm Thoo Talkin'*), a television show (*Diva on a Mission*), a stage play (*We Must Go Forward: The Passion of the Black Man*), and a host of videos and commercials. Jay has appeared on television shows such as The Steve Harvey Show and Oprah Winfrey's show "The Big Give". Jay now resides in Atlanta, Georgia and travels the world speaking to people inspiring them to ***Tap Into Their Destiny***.

Me standing in front of the shop that I walked into after a disagreement with the owner of the previous barbershop.

Me cutting Jalil White's hair

My father and I

Me on the set of my first movie
"Get Right or Get Left"

My vision of possibilities when I Tap Into MY
Destiny.

Me at the Red Carpet screening of my movie "When We Were Kids"

CONTACT

J. White
President/CEO
FISHERS OF MEN PRODUCTIONS LLC
Office: (213) 840-1001
info@tapintoyourdestiny.com
www.tapintoyourdestiny.com
www.fishersofmenproductions.com
www.wemustgoforward.com

Made in the USA
Charleston, SC
29 December 2009